Strictly For Boys

(A Cookbook for Boys 8 to 80)

Betty L. Waskiewicz

P.O. Box 474
Beaufort, SC 29902

INTRODUCTION

This book is written "Strictly for Boys." Just that, good food which boys will enjoy cooking as well as eating.

It has been divided into sections according to the experience needed to prepare. The section for Waterboys will be just right for boys starting out. Then step up to the Junior Varsity, on to the Varsity, and when you get to be a real "Pro" move up to the "All Stars."

Since you will surely want to show off when you get a little more advanced (a disease common among all good cooks), a few fancy things have been included. These will be nice for a special occasion when you want to prepare a meal for Mom and Dad or, "heaven forbid", a girl!!!

Printed in the USA by

WIMMER
The Wimmer Companies, Inc.
Memphis • Dallas

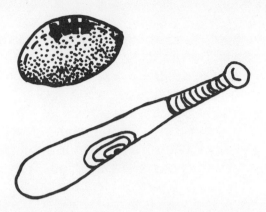

To Lee whose determination to cook without directions led me to try this book, to William who made a good "Guinea Pig", to Lyn who gave the boys the desire to cook, and to their Dad who has the patience of Job and needs it.

This book is a collection of recipes, some original, some contributed by friends, and some adapted from long use by our family.

TABLE OF CONTENTS

TERMS USED IN COOKING

1. **Bacon drippings:** Grease left when bacon is fried or broiled.

2. **Bake:** To cook in the oven.

3. **Broil:** To cook directly under or over heat. Under in the oven, over when using charcoal outside.

4. **Cream:** Mix sugar and shortening until creamy and smooth.

5. **Cut-in:** Mix flour and shortening until it is like coarse sand.

6. **Dash:** The amount added when shaker is given a good shake.

7. **Dredge:** Coat with flour.

8. **Dutch-oven:** Heavy, usually round, sauce pan with heavy lid.

9. **Flute:** To make fancy edge on pie crust.

10. **Fry:** To cook in shortening.

11. **Frying pan:** Shallow, heavy pan with handle used for frying.

12. **Knead:** To work dough back and forth until smooth.

13. **Marinate:** To soak in sauce before cooking.

14. **Meringue:** Egg white beaten stiffly with sugar.

15. **Sauce pan:** A cooking utensil usually having one long handle and a lid.

16. **Sauté:** To cook slowly in melted shortening until tender but not browned.

17. **Scald:** To heat milk until bubbles form around edge of sauce pan.

18. **Scant:** Very level measurement.

19. **Self-rising flour:** Flour which has baking powder and salt added.

20. **Sift:** To put flour through a sifter.

21. **Simmer:** To cook very slowly.

22. **Sprinkle:** To cover lightly.

23. **Stem:** One piece from a stalk of celery.

24. **Stock:** Liquid in which chicken or meat was cooked.

25. **Toss:** Mix by stirring carefully.

SUBSTITUTIONS

Shortening may be used as a substitute for margarine or butter in cake and cookie recipes.

One cup of plain flour with 1 teaspoon of baking powder and ½ teaspoon salt added may be used as a substitute for one cup of self-rising flour.

One half cup of evaporated milk and ½ cup water may be used as a substitute for one cup of whole milk.

Margarine may be used as a substitute for butter.

One tablespoon vinegar added to one cup of milk may be used as a substitute for buttermilk.

HELPFUL HINTS FOR A GOOD COOK

1. Always wash your hands before beginning any task in the kitchen.

2. Read the recipe all the way through before beginning.

3. Make sure you have all ingredients before you begin to cook.

4. Remember to allow plenty of time for preparing and cooking.

5. Measure carefully and follow directions.

6. Always sift flour before measuring.

7. Do not pack flour when measuring.

8. Pack brown sugar tightly when measuring.

9. Put each ingredient away as it is used.

10. Always clean kitchen and wash dishes and utensils when you have finished cooking.

11. Check to see that all switches on stove or oven are off before leaving kitchen.

12. Start out preparing only one part of the meal. Don't try to do too much; as you gain experience in cooking you may do more. When you are really advanced then you may prepare a complete meal.

13. Remember to plan your meal so that the food will be attractive on the plate as well as tasty.

14. You should have a meat, starch, vegetable, salad and a nice dessert.

15. If the meal is heavy, have a light dessert. If the meal is light, you might have a heavier dessert.

SUGGESTED MENUS

Breakfast

Orange juice
Scrambled eggs and bacon
Cinnamon toast
Milk, tea or coffee

Pineapple juice
Blueberry pancakes
Bacon or ham
Milk, tea or coffee

Tomato juice
Curried ham on toast
Milk, tea or coffee

Apple juice
French toast
Bacon, ham or sausage
Milk, tea or coffee

Lunch

Vegetable soup
Corn muffins
Cookies
Milk, tea or coffee

Campout beans
Grilled hot dogs
Sliced pineapple on lettuce
Brownies
Milk, tea or coffee

Happy hamburgers
Lettuce and tomato
Pickles
Baked apples
Milk, tea or coffee

Chicken or tuna salad
Peas
Pickled peaches
Crisp crackers or biscuits
Cherry Cloud
Milk, tea or coffee

Dinner or Supper

Fried chicken
Brown rice
Broccoli
Sliced peaches on lettuce
Baked custard
Milk, tea or coffee

Deviled crab
Hash brown potatoes
Greenbeans supreme
Tossed salad
Lemon meringue pie
Milk, tea or coffee

Pot roast
Potatoes and carrots
Tomato aspic on lettuce
Apple or blueberry pie
Milk, tea or coffee

Chow mein
Mixed fruit on lettuce
Caramel nut rolls
Parfait
Milk, tea or coffee

NOTES

Waterboys

BAKED APPLES
Serves 4

4 cooking apples   1 tablespoon margarine
½ cup sugar
½ teaspoon ground cinnamon

1. Wash and core apples.
2. Place in greased baking dish.
3. Mix sugar and cinnamon, fill the hole in each apple with sugar mixture.
4. Divide the margarine into four parts and place on top of the sugar mixture; cover.
5. Bake at 350° for 45 minutes.

BANANA PUDDING
Serves 6

1 small package vanilla   ½ teaspoon vanilla
  INSTANT pudding   3 ripe bananas
3 cups milk   24 vanilla wafers

1. Peel and slice bananas.
2. Line 2-quart casserole with layer of vanilla wafers; top with a layer of bananas.
3. Make pudding according to directions on package, using 3 cups of milk and adding ½ teaspoon vanilla.
4. Pour ½ pudding over wafers and bananas.
5. Quickly arrange a second layer of wafers and bananas over pudding.
6. Pour remaining pudding over wafers and bananas.
7. Chill about 1 hour before serving.

BROWNIES
Makes 16

⅓ cup shortening
1 cup sugar
2 eggs
⅔ cup self-rising flour

¼ cup cocoa
½ cup nuts, chopped
1 teaspoon vanilla

1. Cream shortening and sugar until light and fluffy.
2. Add eggs; beat well.
3. Add flour, cocoa, nuts, and vanilla.
4. Mix well and pour into well greased 9x9x2-inch pan.
5. Bake at 350° for 20 to 25 minutes.

CHERRY CLOUD PARFAIT
Makes 4 or 5

1 package cherry Jello,
   small size

2 cups non-dairy dessert
   topping

1. Make Jello according to directions on package.
2. Chill until firm but not set.
3 Beat Jello until fluffy, add to bowl with dessert topping and
   beat until well mixed.
4. Pour into parfait glasses and chill for at least 1 hour.
5. Top with a little dessert topping and serve.

This may be used to fill a 9-inch graham cracker crust, topped
with dessert topping, and sprinkled with a few graham cracker
crumbs.

CINNAMON TOAST

½ cup sugar
1 teaspoon ground cinnamon

1. Measure sugar into container, add cinnamon, and mix well. Store in covered container.
2. To make toast spread bread with butter; sprinkle generously with the cinnamon and sugar mixture.
3. Place bread on rack in toaster oven, toast lightly.
4. The cinnamon-sugar mixture keeps well for a long time if kept covered.

CRAB, OYSTER OR SHRIMP COCKTAIL
COCKTAIL SAUCE
Serves 8

1 cup catsup
2 tablespoon lemon juice
2 teaspoons horseradish
2 teaspoons Worcestershire sauce

⅛ teaspoon salt
Dash pepper

1. Mix all ingredients well and chill.
2. Place small pieces of lettuce in cocktail glasses.
3. Add chilled cooked shrimp, lump crab meat, or oysters.
4. Spoon on cocktail sauce.
5. Serve with crisp crackers and lemon wedges.

HARD BOILED EGGS

1. Place eggs in saucepan and cover with water.
2. Bring to a boil, reduce heat, and simmer for 20 minutes.
3. Drain hot water off immediately and cover with cold water; let stand until cool.

POACHED EGG
Serves 1

1 egg   **1 tablespoon margarine**

1. Put margarine in custard cup.
2. Place cup in about 1 inch of water in a saucepan.
3. Heat until water is boiling and margarine is melted.
4. Break egg into cup and gently slide into custard cup.
5. Cover saucepan and boil 3 minutes.
6. Slide egg from custard cup onto buttered toast.

HOT CHOCOLATE
Serves 1

1 cup milk   **2 teaspoons sugar**
1 teaspoon cocoa   **½ teaspoon vanilla**

1. Heat milk, do not boil.
2. Mix cocoa and sugar.
3. Add a little hot milk and stir until smooth.
4. Add to hot milk and stir.
5. Serve in heavy cup and top with marshmallow.

EASY HOT CHOCOLATE
Serves 1

1 cup chocolate milk

1. Heat until hot but not boiling.
2. Serve in heavy cup and top with marshmallow.

HOT DOGS
Serves 4

4 hot dogs   **4 hot dog rolls**

1. Wrap rolls in foil and heat in oven at 350° for 10 minutes.
2. Boil hot dogs in a little water for 5 minutes or fry in margarine in a frying pan for 5 to 8 minutes.
3. Place a hot dog in each warmed roll and top with your favorite relish, mustard, and catsup, or top with chili.

ICED TEA
Serves 8

¼ cup tea leaves   **2 cups water**
1 cup sugar

1. Pour water into saucepan and heat to boiling.
2. Remove from heat and add tea at once.
3. Let this stand about 5 minutes to steep.
4. Put sugar in a 2-quart container.
5. Strain tea over sugar and stir to dissolve.
6. Fill container with cool water.
7. Serve over ice cubes.

LEMONADE
Serves 4

1 lemon, cut in quarters   **⅔ cup sugar**
¼ cup lemon juice, bottled   **Water**
  or canned

1. Wash lemon and cut in quarters.
2. Squeeze lemon into 1-quart container.
3. Add lemon juice, and sugar.
4. Fill container with water and stir until sugar dissolves.
5. To serve, pour over ice cubes in glasses.

OYSTER STEW
Serves 4

½ pint small oysters   2 tablespoons margarine
4 cups whole milk   Salt and pepper to taste

1. Melt margarine in heavy saucepan.
2. Add drained oysters and stir until edges begin to curl.
3. Add milk and heat thoroughly, but do not boil.
4. Salt and pepper to taste.
5. Serve in large bowls with lots of crisp crackers.

PANCAKES
Makes 10

1 cup self-rising flour   2 tablespoons cooking oil
2 tablespoons sugar   ½ cup milk
1 egg

1. Measure flour and sugar into bowl.
2. Add egg, oil, and milk.
3. Stir until flour is just dampened; batter may be lumpy.
4. Pour by the tablespoonful onto hot griddle or frying pan.
5. Let cook until bubbly on top.
6. Turn and cook until second side is lightly browned.
7. Serve with butter and jelly or warm syrup.

Griddle or frying pan is hot enough when a drop of cool water will roll around like a marble, as soon as it is this hot reduce heat to medium. This should keep the temperature right to cook all the pancakes.

BLUEBERRY PANCAKES

1. Wash and drain fresh blueberries.
2. Sprinkle with a little sugar.
3. Add 1 cup blueberries to pancake batter.
4. Cook on hot griddle until top is bubbly.
5. Turn and cook until nicely browned on second side.
6. Serve hot with butter, jelly, or warm syrup.

POTATO SOUP
Serves 6

1 small stem celery, chopped
½ small onion, chopped
1 cup water
2 cups milk
1 chicken bouillon cube

2 tablespoons margarine
½ teaspoon salt
Dash pepper
⅓ cup instant potatoes

1. Melt margarine in heavy saucepan.
2. Add celery and onion, sauté until tender.
3. Add water, milk, bouillon cube, salt, and pepper.
4. Stir until bouillon cube is melted.
5. Slowly stir in the instant potato.
6. Heat thoroughly, but do not boil.
7. Serve in bowls, hot or cold.

Junior Varsity

APPLE MUFFINS
Makes 18

¼ cup shortening
½ cup sugar
1 egg
2½ cups self-rising flour

½ teaspoon nutmeg
½ teaspoon cinnamon
1 cup milk
1 cup chopped apple

1. Cream shortening and sugar until fluffy.
2. Add egg and beat well.
3. Add dry ingredients which have been sifted together.
4. Add apple, then milk, and stir.
5. Fill well-greased muffin pans ½ full.
6. Bake at 375° for 20 to 25 minutes.

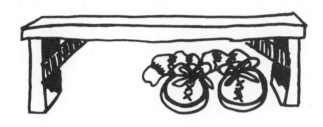

BAKED CUSTARD
Serves 6

2 cups milk
½ cup sugar
2 eggs, beaten

1 teaspoon vanilla
Pinch of salt
Nutmeg, ground

1. Beat eggs well; add sugar, milk, salt and vanilla.
2. Stir until sugar is dissolved.
3. Pour into 6 ovenproof custard cups or a 1-quart baking dish.
4. Sprinkle with nutmeg.
5. Set custard cups or baking dish in a pan and pour about 2 inches of hot water into pan.
6. Bake at 350° about 45 minutes or until lightly browned.
7. Be careful when removing from the oven so as not to spill the hot water.

BANANA CREAM PIE
Serves 8

1 package vanilla INSTANT
  pudding, small
2 cups milk
1 teaspoon vanilla

2 bananas, sliced
2 cups non-dairy whipped
  topping

1. Slice bananas and arrange in bottom of *baked* pie shell.
2. Make pudding according to directions on package, adding 1 teaspoon vanilla.
3. Pour pudding over sliced bananas.
4. Spoon whipped topping carefully over pudding and chill at least 2 hours before serving.

BISCUITS
Makes 16

2 cups self-rising flour
⅓ cup shortening

⅔ cups milk

1. Cut shortening into flour.
2. Add milk and stir until flour is just dampened.
3. Turn onto well-floured surface.
4. Press out to about ½ inch thick.
5. Cut with biscuit cutter and place on ungreased baking sheet.
6. Bake at 450° for about 8 to 10 minutes. Makes about 16.

For cheese biscuits add ½ cup grated sharp cheese to flour and shortening mixture.

SECRET of good biscuits is to handle dough as little as possible.

BREAD PUDDING
Serves 4

4 slices day-old bread
2 eggs, beaten
2 cups milk
½ cup sugar

1 teaspoon vanilla
¼ cup nuts
2 tablespoons raisins

1. Break bread into medium-size pieces.
2. Place in 1-quart casserole; add nuts and raisins.
3. Mix beaten egg, milk, sugar and vanilla.
4. Stir until sugar dissolves.
5. Pour over bread, nuts, and raisins in casserole.
6. Bake at 325° for 30 minutes.

CAMPOUT BEANS
Serves 4

1 No. 2 can pork and beans
2 hot dogs cut in 1 inch
   slices
1 small onion
1 tablespoon shortening

2 tablespoons brown sugar
2 tablespoons catsup
½ teaspoon mustard

1. Peel and cut onion into small pieces.
2. Melt shortening in heavy sauce pan.
3. Add cut onion and fry slowly until tender but not brown.
4. Add remaining ingredients and simmer over low heat 45 minutes.

After onion is tender and ingredients are mixed, these may be poured into a casserole and baked at 350° for 30 minutes.

CARROT, PINEAPPLE AND LIME SALAD
Serves 8

1 3-ounce package lime Jello 2 carrots, grated
1 small can crushed pineapple

1. Drain pineapple well and save the juice.
2. Make Jello according to directions, using pineapple juice as part of the water.
3. Chill until beginning to set.
4. Stir in crushed pineapple and grated carrots.
5. Chill until firm; serve on crisp lettuce leaves, top with a teaspoon of mayonnaise or cream cheese.

GLAZED CARROTS
Serves 4

4 large carrots ½ teaspoon salt
2 tablespoons sugar 2 tablespoons margarine

1. Peel, wash, and slice carrots.
2. Cook in water with salt and 1 tablespoon of sugar.
3. When carrots are tender, drain well.
4. Add margarine and remaining sugar.
5. Heat, stirring carefully, until sugar and margarine are melted and carrots are glazed.

CHEWY CAKE
Makes 16

1 cup brown sugar 1 teaspoon baking powder
2 eggs ¼ teaspoon salt
1 cup plain flour 1 cup pecans, chopped

1. Cook eggs and sugar in top of double boiler until like syrup.
2. Stir in remaining ingredients, mixing well.
3. Pour into well-greased and floured 8 inch square pan.
4. Bake a 325° for 25 minutes.
5. When cool cut into squares.

CHICKEN AND RICE
Serves 5

2 tablespoons margarine
½ small onion, chopped
¼ small bell pepper,
   chopped
1 stem celery, chopped

1 cup raw rice
1 cup diced cooked chicken
¼ teaspoon salt
2 cups chicken stock
Dash pepper

1. Melt margarine in heavy saucepan.
2. Add onion, bell pepper, and celery; cover and cook slowly until tender.
3. Add rice, chicken, stock, salt, and pepper.
4. Cover, bring to a boil, reduce heat and simmer, stirring occasionally until liquid is gone and rice is tender. About 30 minutes.

To make a quick version of this use 2 cups water, 2 chicken bouillon cubes, and a small can of boned chicken.

CHICKEN SOUP
Serves 4

2 cups chicken stock
2 tablespoons raw rice
Salt and pepper to taste

1 cup cooked chicken,
   finely cut

1. Bring stock to a boil in heavy saucepan.
2. Add chicken and rice.
3. Bring to a boil; add salt and pepper.
4. Reduce heat and simmer about 30 to 40 minutes.

CHOCOLATE CHIP COOKIES
Makes 5 dozen

½ cup shortening
¾ cup sugar
1 egg
1¼ cups flour
1 teaspoon vanilla

½ teaspoon salt
½ teaspoon soda
1 cup chocolate chips
1 cup nuts, chopped

1. Cream shortening and sugar until fluffy.
2. Add egg and beat well.
3. Add flour, salt, soda, vanilla, chips, and nuts.
4. Stir well; dough will be very stiff.
5. Drop by the teaspoonful on greased cookie sheets.
6. Bake at 375° for 8 to 10 minutes or until lightly browned.

CHOCOLATE FROSTING
Fills and frosts 9 inch layer cake

1 pound of 10X confectioners
    sugar
⅓ cup oleo or shortening
½ cup cocoa

Pinch salt
½ cup milk
1 teaspoon vanilla
½ cup chopped nuts

1. Put all ingredients except nuts into small mixer bowl.
2. Mix at low speed until blended.
3. Mix at high speed until light and fluffy.
4. Spread on top of layer, add second layer, spread frosting on this layer.
5. Frost sides and top of cake and sprinkle with chopped nuts.

COCONUT CREAM PIE
Serves 8

1 package vanilla INSTANT
  pudding, small
2 cups milk
1 teaspoon vanilla

1 cup coconut
2 cups non-dairy whipped
  topping

1. Make instant pudding according to directions on package adding vanilla and coconut.
2. Pour into 9 inch *baked* pie shell.
3. Spread with whipped topping. Sprinkle with a little additional coconut.
4. Chill well before serving.

CORN MUFFINS
Makes 18

1½ cups yellow corn meal
½ cup flour
1 teaspoon salt
4 teaspoons baking powder

¼ cup cooking oil
¼ cup sugar
2 eggs, beaten
1 cup milk

1. Mix corn meal, flour, salt, sugar, and baking powder.
2. Add milk, eggs, and oil.
3. Stir until just blended.
4. Fill well greased muffin pans ½ full.
5. Bake at 425° for 20 minutes.

CREAM CHEESE PIE
Serves 8

1 8-ounce package cream
  cheese
2 cups non-dairy whipped
  topping

1 can prepared cherry pie
  filling

1. Beat cream cheese in small bowl until soft and fluffy.
2. Add cream cheese to whipped topping and beat until well blended.
3. Pour into 9 inch graham cracker crust and chill for ½ hour.
4. Carefully spoon cherry pie filling over cream cheese mixture and chill at least 2 hours before serving.

Blueberry, peach, or strawberry pie filling may be used as a substitute for cherry pie filling.

DREAM SANDWICH
Makes 4

4 slices of white bread
4 slices of American cheese
4 large tomato slices

4 slices of bacon
Mayonnaise

1. Spread each slice of bread with mayonnaise.
2. Add a slice of cheese.
3. Add tomato slice.
4. Cut each bacon slice in half and lay over the tomato.
5. Place on baking sheet and bake at 350° for 10 minutes.
6. Then broil for 5 minutes until bacon is brown.
7. Serve hot.

FRIED EGG
Serves 1

1 egg   **1 tablespoon margarine**

1. Heat margarine in frying pan.
2. Break egg into cup.
3. Slide carefully into melted margarine.
4. Fry until the egg begins to get firm.
5. Turn gently and fry on other side.
6. If you like your egg hard, fry longer.
7. For sunnyside up do not turn, but spoon melted margarine over the top once or twice; remove from pan.

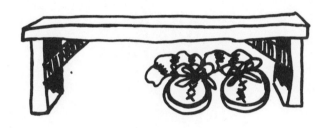

MAN ON A RAFT
Serves 1

1 slice bread   **1 egg**

1. Grease and heat frying pan.
2. With biscuit cutter or glass cut circle in center of bread.
3. Put bread into frying pan add circle on one side.
4. Break egg into cup and gently slip into hole in center of bread.
5. Cook until egg is beginning to get firm.
6. Gently turn over and cook until egg is as cooked as you like.
7. Serve with bacon, ham or sausage, and the circle from the center.

EGG SALAD SANDWICH
Makes 2

1 egg
2 tablespoons mayonnaise
½ teaspoon pickle relish

Salt and pepper to taste
2 slices sandwich bread

1. Place egg in small saucepan; cover with water.
2. Bring to boil, reduce heat, and simmer for 20 minutes.
3. Pour off hot water and cover with cold water; let stand until cool.
4. Peel and mash with a fork until fine.
5. Add mayonnaise, pickle relish, salt and pepper; mix well.
6. Spread on one slice of bread; top with remaining slice.
7. For fancy sandwich trim off crust and cut into four small pieces.

SCRAMBLED EGGS AND BACON
Serves 1

2 slices bacon
1 egg, beaten
2 tablespoons milk

Pinch of salt
Dash of pepper

1. Place bacon in heavy frying pan.
2. Fry on medium heat until lightly brown, turning one time.
3. Remove from pan and drain on paper towels.
4. Beat egg with milk, salt, and pepper.
5. Reduce heat under pan; drain bacon dripping from pan.
6. Pour egg into pan and cook slowly, stirring until egg is as firm as you like.
7. Serve with bacon and toast on a warm plate.

FLOATING ISLAND
Serves 6

1 small package vanilla
  INSTANT pudding
2½ cups milk
½ teaspoon vanilla

1 cup prunes
2 egg whites
4 tablespoons confectioners
  sugar

1. Stew prunes by directions on package, pit and mash.
2. Make pudding according to directions on package, using 2½ cups milk and ½ teaspoon vanilla.
3. Beat egg whites until soft peaks form, add sugar, and continue beating until very stiff.
4. Fold mashed prunes into beaten egg whites.
5. Spoon a little pudding into 6 dessert dishes.
6. Add some of the egg white-prune mixture.
7. Pour the remaining pudding over prune mixture.
8. Top with a little of the remaining prune mixture.

FRENCH TOAST
Makes 3 slices

1 egg, beaten
½ cup milk
Pinch of salt

½ teaspoon sugar
3 slices white bread

1. Mix egg, milk, salt, and sugar.
2. Pour into low flat bowl.
3. Dip bread, one piece at a time, into egg mixture; turn over.
4. Carefully lift out bread and place in hot, greased frying pan.
5. Brown lightly on one side, turn, and brown the second side.
6. Serve hot with butter and jelly or warm syrup.

QUICK FRUIT COBBLER
Serves 6

½ cup self-rising flour
½ cup sugar
½ cup milk

2 tablespoons margarine
1 No. 2 can blueberries,
    peaches, or cherries

1. Melt margarine in 1-quart baking dish.
2. Mix flour, sugar, and milk.
3. Pour slowly into baking dish.
4. Carefully pour the fruit into the center of the flour mixture.
5. Bake at 350° for 30 minutes or until lightly browned.

To make this with fresh fruit, use 2 cups fruit which have been sprinkled with sugar and left standing for about 30 minutes to form a syrup.

GINGERBREAD
Serves 8

¼ cup shortening
½ cup brown sugar
1 egg
½ cup molasses

½ cup milk
2½ cups self-rising flour
½ teaspoon ground ginger
½ teaspoon cinnamon

1. Cream sugar and shortening.
2. Add egg and beat well.
3. Sift flour, ginger, and cinnamon together.
4. Mix milk and molasses.
5. Add sifted flour and milk mixture alternately to the creamed sugar, shortening, and egg mixture.
6. Mix well and pour into a well greased 9 inch square pan.
7. Bake at 350° for 25 minutes.
8. Serve warm, topped with lemon sauce or whipped cream.

GRAHAM CRACKER CRUST
Makes 1 crust

18 graham crackers, finely crushed

¼ cup melted margarine
⅓ cup sugar

1. Crush crackers by placing in a plastic bag and rolling with a rolling pin.
2. Mix crumbs, margarine, and sugar well.
3. Pack firmly into 9 inch pie pan, bottom and sides.
4. Bake at 350° for 5 minutes or chill well before filling.

GREEN BEANS SUPREME
Serves 4

1 No. 2 can French style green beans
1 4-oz. can mushroom pieces

2 tablespoons sliced almonds or pecans
2 tablespoons chopped onion
2 tablespoons margarine

1. Heat beans in their own liquid.
2. Sauté onions, mushrooms, and nuts in margarine until onion is tender.
3. Drain beans well and add to pan with onion and mushrooms.
4. Stir well until all liquid is gone.

GRILLED CHEESE SANDWICH
Makes 2

2 slices cheese
4 slices sandwich bread

Margarine

1. Spread each slice of bread with margarine.
2. Put a slice of cheese between two slices of bread.
3. Place in hot sandwich grill and brown.
4. If no sandwich grill is available, place sandwiches in warm frying pan greased with a little margarine.
5. Brown on one side; turn and brown on second side.
6. Serve hot.

HAMBURGER STEAKS
Makes 4

1 pound hamburger
1 teaspoon salt
Dash pepper

1 large onion, chopped
2 tablespoons flour
2 tablespoons shortening

1. Mix meat, ½ teaspoon salt, and pepper and form into 4 large patties.
2. Heat shortening in 9 inch heavy frying pan.
3. Sauté onion until tender, remove to small dish.
4. Brown meat on both sides; remove from pan.
5. Add flour to drippings in pan; stir until lightly browned.
6. Carefully add 1 cup water, ½ teaspoon salt, and dash of pepper, stirring constantly until thickened. (Watch out for rising steam.)
7. Return meat and onions to pan with gravy, cover, and simmer very slowly for 30 minutes.

CURRIED HAM
Serves 6

1 cup cooked ham, cut in
** cubes**
2 cups milk
½ teaspoon salt

1 teaspoon curry powder
2 tablespoons margarine
2 tablespoons flour
Dash of pepper

1. Melt margarine, add flour and curry powder, stir well.
2. Slowly add milk and cook over medium heat until thickened, stirring constantly.
3. Add salt, pepper, and ham.
4. Serve hot on toast.

HAPPY HAMBURGERS
Makes 6

1 pound of hamburger
½ cup Rice Krispies
1 teaspoon salt
¼ scant teaspoon pepper

Dash of garlic salt
¼ cup milk
1 egg, beaten

1. Put all ingredients in a medium size bowl.
2. Mix well with your CLEAN hand.
3. Shape into 6 patties.
4. Put in hot frying pan and fry until brown on one side.
5. Turn and fry on second side until done.
6. Serve in heated hamburger bun with your favorite trimmings.

MONDAY'S HASH
Serves 2

1 cup left-over roast, cubed
1 medium potato, peeled and
   diced
1 small onion, chopped

2 cups gravy (Use leftover
   gravy with enough water
   to make 2 cups.)
Salt and pepper to taste

1. Place all ingredients in heavy saucepan.
2. Bring to a boil, reduce heat, and simmer about 30 minutes.

If there is no gravy left, use 2 cups water and 2 beef bouillon cubes.

HAYSTACKS
Makes 2 dozen

1 cup Chinese Chow Mein
   noodles
1 6-ounce package butterscotch
   chips

½ cup chopped nuts or
   salted peanuts

1. Melt chips in top of double boiler, over hot water.
2. Remove from heat and stir in noodles and nuts.
3. Mix well and drop by teaspoonsful on greased cookie sheet.
4. Let stand until firm.

Chocolate chips may be used instead of the butterscotch chips.

34

HOT DOGS, STUFFED
Serves 6

6 hot dogs
1 cup grated sharp cheese

½ cup chili sauce
6 slices bacon

1. Mix chili and cheese.
2. Split hot dogs almost through.
3. Fill split with cheese mixture.
4. Wrap hot dog with bacon slice, pin each end with toothpick.
5. Place on pan and broil until bacon is brown, about 5 minutes.

ICE CREAM CAKE
Serves 12

1 angel food loaf cake,
  about 12x4x3
1 quart ice cream

8 oz. non-dairy whipped
  topping

1. Slice loaf cake long way into two layers.
2. Spoon slightly softened ice cream on bottom half.
3. Replace top half and put in freezer until chilled.
4. Spread the whipped topping over the top and sides of the chilled cake.
5. Return to freezer until ready to serve.

If strawberry ice cream is used, top with a few fresh or frozen strawberries before serving.

If chocolate ice cream is used, drizzle top with chocolate syrup before serving.

Two or three drops of food coloring may be added to the whipped topping for a more attractive topping.

LEMON SAUCE
Serves 8

¼ cup lemon juice
¾ cup water
¼ cup sugar
1 tablespoon cornstarch

2 tablespoons margarine
3 drops yellow food
   coloring
Dash salt

1. Mix lemon juice, water, cornstarch, and sugar in saucepan.
2. Stir until well blended; add margarine and food coloring.
3. Cook over medium heat, stirring constantly until thickened and clear.
4. Serve over warm gingerbread.

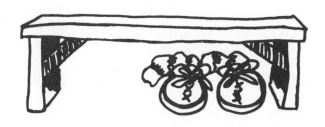

LIME AND CREAM CHEESE SALAD
Serves 8

1 small can crushed
   pineapple
1 3-ounce package lime Jello

1 3-ounce package cream
   cheese
½ cup chopped nuts

1. Drain pineapple well and save juice.
2. Make Jello according to directions, using pineapple juice as part of the water.
3. Mix a little of the Jello with the cream cheese and stir until cheese is softened.
4. Stir cheese mixture into remaining Jello.
5. Chill until beginning to set; stir in crushed pineapple and chopped nuts.
6. Chill until firm; serve on crisp lettuce leaves.
7. Top with a little mayonnaise sprinkled with a few chopped nuts.

MACARONI AND CHEESE
Serves 6

4 ounces elbow macaroni
8 ounces sharp Cheddar
  cheese, grated
2 cups milk

2 eggs, beaten
½ teaspoon salt
2 tablespoons margarine
Dash of pepper

1. Boil and drain macaroni by directions on package.
2. Pour drained macaroni into 1½-quart baking dish.
3. Mix cheese with cooked macaroni.
4. Beat eggs, add milk, salt, pepper, and margarine, mix well.
5. Pour over macaroni and cheese in baking dish.
6. Bake at 350° about 30 minutes or until firm.

PARFAIT
Serves 6

1 package vanilla INSTANT
  pudding, small
1 package chocolate INSTANT
  pudding, small

1 teaspoon vanilla
4 cups milk

1. Make vanilla pudding according to directions on package, adding ½ teaspoon vanilla.
2. Make chocolate pudding according to directions on package, adding ½ teaspoon vanilla.
3. Fill parfait glasses with alternate layers of vanilla and chocolate pudding.
4. Top with dessert topping and a few chopped nuts or graham cracker crumbs.
5. Chill well before serving.

PINEAPPLE UPSIDE-DOWN CAKE
Serves 8

1 yellow or white cake mix
  for single layer
¼ cup margarine
½ cup brown sugar
1 small can crushed pineapple

12 maraschino cherries, cut
  in quarters
¼ cup pecans, chopped

1. Drain pineapple; save juice.
2. Melt margarine in 9 inch layer cake pan.
3. Sprinkle brown sugar, cherries, nuts and pineapple over margarine.
4. Mix cake according to directions on package, using pineapple juice as part of water.
5. Pour into pan and spread gently to edges.
6. Bake at 350° for 25 minutes or until cake springs back when touched lightly in center.
7. Serve warm topped with dessert topping.

QUICK PIZZA
Serves 4

4 slices bread
½ cup pizza sauce, canned

½ cup sharp cheese, grated
4 slices bacon

1. Sprinkle the bread with ½ of the grated cheese.
2. Divide the sauce equally between the 4 slices of bread and spread.
3. Sprinkle with remaining cheese.
4. Cut bacon in small pieces and lay on top of cheese.
5. Broil until bacon is brown and cheese is bubbling.

HASH BROWN POTATOES
Serves 6

4 medium potatoes   ½ teaspoon salt
½ small onion, chopped   Pepper
¼ cup melted shortening

1. Peel, wash, and cube potatoes.
2. Boil potatoes and onion in salted water until tender.
3. Drain potatoes well.
4. Melt shortening in heavy frying pan.
5. Add potatoes and onions, and fry until brown and crisp.
6. Sprinkle with pepper and serve hot.

POTATO SALAD
Serves 4

4 medium potatoes   ⅓ cup mayonnaise
2 eggs, hard boiled   Salt and pepper to taste
2 tablespoons pickle, chopped

1. Peel, wash, and dice potatoes.
2. Boil potatoes in salted water until just tender.
3. Drain at once and let cool.
4. In large bowl mix potatoes, chopped boiled egg, mayonnaise, pickle, salt, and pepper.
5. Mix well and chill.

BROWN RICE
Serves 6

⅔ cup rice   1 can onion soup
2 tablespoons margarine ½ soup can of water
1 4-ounce can mushroom
  pieces, drained

1. Melt margarine in heavy saucepan.
2. Add rice and mushroom pieces.
3. Brown rice and mushrooms in melted margarine, stirring often.
4. Add soup and water; bring to boiling.
5. Reduce heat, cover, and simmer, stirring occasionally until rice is tender, about 25 minutes.

RICE PUDDING
Serves 6

1 cup cooked rice
2 cups milk
½ cup sugar
2 eggs, beaten

½ cup raisins or chopped
nuts
1 teaspoon vanilla

1. Beat eggs; stir in sugar until dissolved.
2. Mix in rice, milk, raisins or nuts and vanilla.
3. Pour into greased 1½-quart baking dish.
4. Bake at 325° for 40 minutes; stir gently with a fork after the first 15 minutes.

RED RICE
Serves 6

1 stem celery, chopped
½ medium bell pepper,
chopped
1 small onion, chopped
2 tablespoons margarine
1 cup raw rice

2 cups canned tomatoes
1 teaspoon salt
⅛ teaspoon pepper
2 or 3 tablespoons ham
drippings

1. In heavy saucepan, sauté celery, bell pepper and onion in margarine until tender, but not brown.
2. Add rice, tomatoes, salt, pepper, and ham drippings.
3. Bring to boiling, cover, reduce heat and simmer until rice is tender, about 30 minutes.
4. Stir carefully several times during cooking.

(Ham drippings—the good brown stock left in the pan after ham is baked.)

COUNTRY STEW
Serves 4

1 pound boneless stew meat
1 quart water
4 medium potatoes
2 medium onions

4 large carrots
1 teaspoon salt
Dash pepper
1 beef bouillon cube

1. Bring water to boil in large saucepan.
2. Add meat, salt, pepper, and bouillon cube.
3. Cover and simmer while preparing vegetables.
4. Peel and quarter potatoes, onions, and carrots.
5. Wash and add to cooking meat.
6. Bring to a boil, reduce heat, and simmer at least 1 and ½ hours.

Serve with a tossed salad and corn muffins for a nice hot meal.

CRAB STEW
Serves 4

1 cup fresh crab meat or 1
  6-ounce can of crab meat
¼ cup margarine
½ small onion, chopped
½ stem celery, chopped or
  ¼ teaspoon celery seed

2 tablespoons flour
2½ cups milk
½ teaspoon salt
Dash pepper

1. Melt margarine in heavy saucepan.
2. Add chopped onion and celery and sauté until tender but not brown.
3. Add crab meat and stir for a minute or two.
4. Sprinkle flour over crab meat and stir well.
5. Add milk and stir constantly until thickened.
6. Serve in bowls with crisp crackers.

SHRIMP STEW
Serves 4

1 cup shrimp (boiled and
  peeled)
¼ cup margarine
½ small onion, chopped
1 small stem celery, chopped

2 tablespoons flour
2 cups milk
½ teaspoon salt
Dash pepper

1. Melt margarine in heavy saucepan.
2. Add onion and celery and sauté until tender and slightly browned.
3. Add flour and stir well.
4. Add milk and stir constantly until thickened.
5. Add shrimp and heat thoroughly but do not boil
6. Serve over rice or toast.

POOR BOY'S STROGANOFF
Serves 4

1 pound boneless chuck stew
1 can cream of mushroom
  soup
1 package dry onion soup mix

4 ounces wide egg noodles
1 tablespoon margarine
¼ cup sour cream

1. Mix meat and soups well and pour into oven-proof casserole.
2. Cover tightly and bake at 350° for 1½ hours.
3. Twenty minutes before meat is done, cook noodles according to directions on package.
4. When noodles are done, drain well and add margarine; stir well.
5. When meat is done, stir in the cooked noodles.
6. Just before serving stir in the sour cream.

TOMATO ASPIC
Serves 4

2 cups tomato juice
1 envelope gelatin, unflavored
1 tablespoon lemon juice
Dash of salt

Dash of pepper
½ teaspoon Worcestershire
  sauce

1. Sprinkle gelatin on ½ cup tomato juice and stir until dissolved.
2. Heat remaining juice, add dissolved gelatin, lemon juice, salt, pepper, and Worcestershire sauce.
3. Pour into four ½ cup molds and place in refrigerator until firm.
4. Serve on crisp lettuce leaf topped with a little mayonnaise and an olive.

JUNIOR VARSITY

TUNA CASSEROLE
Serves 4

1 6-ounce can tuna
1 can cream of mushroom
   soup
½ cup milk

1 cup potato chips, slightly
   crushed
1 cup cooked green peas

1. Mix all ingredients together.
2. Pour into 1-quart casserole dish.
3. Sprinkle additional crushed potato chips over top.
4. Bake at 350° for 20 to 25 minutes.

TUNA SALAD
Serves 4

1 6-ounce can tuna, drained
2 hard boiled eggs, chopped
2 tablespoons pickles,
   chopped

¼ cup mayonnaise or salad
   dressing
Salt and pepper to taste

1. Crumble tuna in a medium bowl.
2. Add remaining ingredients and mix well.
3. Chill well and serve on lettuce leaves.

TUNA SALAD FOR SIX

1 cup of spaghetti,
   broken into small pieces

2 tablespoons mayonnaise

1. Cook spaghetti according to directions on package.
2. Drain well.
3. Add drained spaghetti and mayonnaise to tuna salad mixture for four. Chill well.

VEGETABLE SOUP
Serves 8

1 ham bone or ham hock
1 quart water
1 No. 2 can tomatoes
1 8-ounce can tomato sauce
1 large potato, peeled and
  diced
1 medium onion, chopped

1 10-ounce package frozen
  mixed vegetables
½ 10-ounce package cut
  okra
1 teaspoon salt
Dash of pepper

1. Boil ham bone or hock in water in large, covered saucepan
   for 1 hour.
2. Add tomatoes, sauce, potato, onion, mixed vegetables,
   okra, salt, and pepper.
3. Bring to a boil, cover, reduce heat, and simmer for 1 hour or
   longer.
4. Serve hot with corn muffins.

WAFFLES
Makes 6

2 cups self-rising flour
¼ cup sugar
¼ cup cooking oil

2 eggs, beaten
1 cup milk

1. Measure sugar and flour into medium bowl.
2. Add oil, eggs and milk.
3. Stir until just blended.
4. Bake in hot waffle iron until golden brown.
5. Serve hot with butter and syrup or jelly.

WHIPPED CREAM
Makes 2 cups

1 cup whipping cream
2 tablespoons confectioners
  sugar

½ teaspoon vanilla

1. Whip the cream at high mixer speed until soft peaks begin
   to form. (Do not overbeat.)
2. Stir in sugar and vanilla; chill thoroughly.

APPLE PIE
Serves 8

7 large tart apples
½ cup sugar
¼ cup brown sugar
2 tablespoons tapioca

1 tablespoon cornstarch
½ teaspoon cinnamon
2 tablespoons margarine

1. Peel and slice apples; add sugar, tapioca, cornstarch, and cinnamon.
2. Mix well and pour into *unbaked* 9 inch pie shell.
3. Dot with margarine; top with unbaked crust.
4. Flute edges, prick top and bake at 450° for 10 minutes. Reduce heat and continue baking at 350° for 30 to 40 minutes.

BLUEBERRY MUFFINS
Makes 18

2 cups self-rising flour
¼ cup sugar
¼ cup shortening,
  melted

1 cup milk
2 eggs
1 cup fresh blueberries
2 tablespoons sugar

1. Wash berries and drain well; sprinkle with 2 tablespoons sugar.
2. Mix flour and sugar; add eggs, milk, and shortening.
3. Stir until flour mixture is just dampened.
4. Stir in berries.
5. Fill greased muffin pans half full.
6. Bake at 350° for about 20 minutes.

BLUEBERRY PIE
Serves 8

1 quart blueberries
1 cup sugar
2 tablespoons cornstarch
3 tablespoons tapioca

¼ teaspoon salt
¼ teaspoon nutmeg
2 tablespoons margarine

1. Wash and drain berries.
2. Put berries in large bowl; add sugar, cornstarch, tapioca, and nutmeg.
3. Mix well and pour into *unbaked* 9 inch pie shell.
4. Dot with margarine.
5. Top with crust; flute edges, prick top.
6. Bake at 450° for 10 minutes; reduce heat to 350° and bake 40 minutes longer.

BOSTON CREAM PIE
Serves 8

1 yellow cake mix for single layer
1 package vanilla INSTANT pudding, small

1½ teaspoons vanilla

Glaze:

1 cup confectioners sugar
1 tablespoon margarine
¼ cup cocoa

3 tablespoons milk
½ teaspoon vanilla

1. Make cake by directions on package, adding ½ teaspoon vanilla; bake and cool.
2. Split cake into two thin layers.
3. Make pudding by directions on package, adding 1 teaspoon vanilla; let stand until firm.
4. Place bottom half of cake layer, cut side up, on plate.
5. Spread ½ of the pudding almost to the edge of the layer.
6. Top with remaining layer, cut side down.
7. Mix glaze ingredients and stir until smooth.
8. Spread glaze over top of cake; when glaze hardens dust with a little confectioners sugar.
9. Chill before serving.

CAROLINA TRIFLE
Serves 8

1 small package vanilla
 INSTANT pudding
½ 9-inch cake layer
¾ cup grated coconut

3 cups milk
1 teaspoon vanilla
8 oz. non-dairy whipped
 topping

1. Crumble ½ of the cake into a 10x6x2 inch casserole.
2. Sprinkle with ¼ cup coconut.
3. Make pudding according to directions, using the 3 cups milk and 1 teaspoon vanilla.
4. Pour ½ of the pudding immediately over the crumbled cake and coconut.
5. Quickly crumble remaining cake over the pudding and sprinkle with ¼ cup coconut.
6. Pour remaining pudding over the cake and coconut.
7. Spread whipped topping over pudding; sprinkle with remaining coconut.
8. Chill at least 2 hours before serving.

CHERRY PIE
Serves 8

1 No. 303 can of red pitted
 cherries
½ cup sugar
2 tablespoons cornstarch

2 tablespoons margarine
½ teaspoon red food
 coloring

1. Drain cherry juice into cup and add enough water to make ¾ cup.
2. Pour into saucepan, add sugar, cornstarch, margarine, and food coloring.
3. Cook, stirring constantly until thick and clear.
4. Add cherries and pour into *unbaked* 9 inch pie shell.
5. Top with crust; prick top.
6. Flute edges and bake at 450° for 10 minutes, reduce heat to 350°, and bake for additional 25 minutes.

BROILED CHICKEN
Serves 4

1 3-pound broiler-fryer   1 teaspoon salt
2 tablespoons melted butter

1. Have chicken cut down front, and press down flat.
2. Wash well and drain.
3. Sprinkle with salt and let stand about an hour.
4. Place chicken on broiler rack, cut side up.
5. Brush with melted margarine.
6. Place broiler pan on lowest rack in oven.
7. Broil for 20 minutes, turn and brush with melted margarine.
8. Broil for 20 minutes.
9. Cover tightly with aluminum foil.
10. Bake at 350° for 20 minutes.

CURRIED CHICKEN
Serves 6

2 cups chicken stock   1 teaspoon curry powder
2 cups cooked chicken, cut   ½ tart apple, peeled and
   into cubes   chopped
¼ cup flour   ½ teaspoon salt
¼ cup margarine   Dash pepper

1. Melt margarine; stir in flour and curry powder.
2. Add stock and cook over medium heat until thick and clear.
3. Add chicken and apple; heat thoroughly. Serve over cooked
   rice.

Be sure to serve toasted coconut and toasted slivered almonds with this dish.

CHICKEN SALAD
Serves 4

2 cups cooked chicken,   2 stems celery, chopped
   cubed   2 tablespoons pickle,
2 boiled eggs, chopped   chopped
¼ cup mayonnaise   Salt and pepper to taste

1. Mix all ingredients together.
2. Chill well and serve on lettuce leaves.

For a little change add ¼ cup chopped peanuts or pecans to
salad.

CHICKEN SALAD SANDWICHES

1. Spread salad between slices of fresh bread.
2. Cut into halves or quarters.

SMOTHERED CHICKEN
Serves 6

1 3-pound broiler-fryer, cut up	1 cup flour
1 teaspoon salt	2 tablespoons margarine
1 can cream of mushroom soup	Dash of pepper
½ soup can of water	

1. Wash and drain chicken, sprinkle with salt, and let stand 1 hour.
2. Put flour and pepper in plastic bag; add 2 or 3 pieces of chicken at a time and shake until well coated with flour; continue until all chicken is floured.
3. Place floured chicken, skin side up, in 9x12x2 inch casserole.
4. Sprinkle with remaining flour.
5. Mix soup with water, pour over chicken, and dot with margarine.
6. Cover tightly with aluminum foil and bake at 350° for 1¼ hours.

CHILI FOR HOT DOGS
Enough for 12 hot dogs

1 pound hamburger	½ teaspoon chili powder
2 8-ounce cans tomato sauce	Dash of pepper
1 small onion, chopped	1 tablespoon brown sugar
1 teaspoon salt	

1. Brown meat in heavy 9 inch frying pan, stirring so that it breaks apart.
2. When meat is brown, use slotted spoon to spoon it into a heavy saucepan.
3. Add all other ingredients and simmer about 30 minutes.
4. Serve over cooked hot dogs in heated buns.

CHILI WITH BEANS
Serves 6

1 pound hamburger
1 No. 2 can tomatoes
1 8-ounce can tomato sauce
1 small onion, chopped
½ bell pepper, chopped
2 stems celery, chopped

1 No. 2 can kidney beans
1 teaspoon salt
Dash pepper
1 teaspoon chili powder
1 tablespoon cooking oil

1. Brown meat and onion in oil in heavy frying pan.
2. Stir while browning so that meat breaks apart.
3. When brown, use slotted spoon to transfer meat to heavy saucepan.
4. Add all other ingredients, except beans; bring to a boil, reduce heat and simmer for 1 hour, stirring occasionally.
5. Add beans and heat thoroughly.
6. Serve hot in bowls with crisp crackers.

CHOCOLATE CAKE
Makes 2 or 3 9-inch layers

1 cup Crisco
2 cups sugar
3 cups flour
4 eggs
1 cup milk

½ cup cocoa
½ teaspoon salt
3 scant teaspoons baking powder
1 teaspoon vanilla

1. Cream sugar and Crisco.
2. Add eggs, two at a time and mix well.
3. Sift together flour, baking powder, salt, and cocoa.
4. Add to creamed mixture alternately with milk and vanilla, beginning with dry ingredients.
5. Bake in well-greased and floured layer pans at 325° for 30 minutes.
6. If baked in three layers, bake about 20 minutes.
7. Fill and frost with chocolate or boiled white frosting.

CHOCOLATE FUDGE
Makes 25 squares

2 cups sugar
½ cup cocoa
1 cup milk
2 tablespoons margarine

Dash salt
1 teaspoon vanilla
½ cup chopped nuts

1. Mix cocoa, sugar, and milk.
2. Cook over low heat until a soft boil forms, 232° on a candy thermometer.
3. Remove from heat and let cool for about 5 minutes.
4. Add margarine, vanilla, and nuts, and beat until thick and creamy.
5. Pour into greased 8x8 inch pan.
6. Let cool and cut into squares.

CHOP SUEY-CHOW MEIN
Serves 6

1 pound round steak, cut in thin strips
1 medium onion, sliced
2 stems celery, sliced
½ teaspoon salt
Dash of pepper
½ cup cooking oil

1 No. 2 can Chinese vegetables
1 8-ounce can water chestnuts, sliced
3 cups water
3 beef bouillon cubes
2 tablespoons soy sauce
3 tablespoons cornstarch

1. Heat oil in heavy saucepan and brown meat quickly.
2. Add bouillon cubes to 2½ cups water and bring to boiling, add browned meat, cover, and simmer for 20 minutes.
3. Add onions, celery, salt, and pepper; simmer for 10 minutes.
4. Rinse Chinese vegetables and chestnuts in cold water, drain well, and add to saucepan. Heat thoroughly.
5. Mix cornstarch with remaining ½ cup water, stir into cooking meat and vegetables, add soy sauce and cook, stirring constantly until thickened and clear.
6. For Chop Suey serve over cooked rice; for Chow Mein serve over Chinese noodles.

For Chicken Chow Mein or Chop Suey:
Substitute 3 cups chicken stock for water and bouillon cubes.
Substitute 2 cups diced cooked chicken for round steak.

CINNAMON COFFEE CAKE
Serves 6

3 cups self-rising flour
½ cup shortening
½ cup sugar
1 egg, beaten
Milk

4 tablespoons margarine
½ cup brown sugar
¼ cup nuts, chopped
Ground cinnamon

1. Cut shortening into flour and sugar.
2. Beat egg, pour into cup, and fill with milk.
3. Add milk and egg to dry ingredients and stir until flour is dampened.
4. Press out on floured surface to a 9 x 15 inch rectangle.
5. Brush with 2 tablespoons melted margarine and sprinkle with ¼ cup brown sugar, nuts, and cinnamon.
6. Roll up as a jelly roll; cut into 15 slices.
7. Pour 2 tablespoons melted oleo into 9 inch round pan; sprinkle with ¼ cup brown sugar.
8. Lay slices on top of the melted margarine and brown sugar.
9. Bake at 375° for 30 minutes.
10. Remove from oven; quickly run knife blade around edge of pan. Place rack over pan and turn over quickly; remove pan.
11. When cool, frost top with confectioners icing.

CONFECTIONERS ICING

1 cup confectioners sugar
1 tablespoon margarine

2 tablespoons milk
¼ teaspoon vanilla

1. Mix sugar and margarine, add milk and vanilla, stir until smooth.
2. Spread over top of Coffee Cake.

COCONUT CUSTARD PIE
Serves 8

2 cups milk	Dash salt
⅔ cup sugar	1 cup grated coconut
3 eggs	1 teaspoon vanilla

1. Beat eggs, add sugar, and stir until dissolved.
2. Scald milk and add to sugar and eggs.
3. Add salt, vanilla, and coconut, mix well.
4. Pour into chilled *unbaked* pie shell.
5. Bake at 400° for 25 minutes.

COCONUT MERINGUE PIE
Serves 8

1 package vanilla pudding and pie mix (not instant), small	1 teaspoon vanilla
2 cups milk	6 tablespoons sugar
3 eggs, separated	1 cup grated coconut

1. Cook pudding according to directions on package, adding the 3 beaten egg yolks.
2. Cool and add vanilla and coconut. Save a little coconut for top.
3. Pour into 9 inch *baked* pie shell.
4. Top with meringue; sprinkle with remaining coconut.
5. Bake at 300° for 30 minutes.

MERINGUE

1. Beat 3 egg whites until peaks begin to form.
2. Gradually add 6 tablespoons sugar and continue beating until very stiff.

COCONUT FROSTING
Fills and frosts 9 inch layer cake

1 recipe of fluffy white frosting

1½ cups grated coconut

1. Spread fluffy white frosting between layers, on top and sides.
2. Sprinkle coconut between layers, on sides and top.

FLUFFY WHITE FROSTING
Fills and frosts 9 inch layer cake

1½ cups sugar
½ cup water
¼ teaspoon cream of tartar
Pinch of salt

3 egg whites
1 teaspoon vanilla
3 tablespoons confectioners sugar

1. Mix sugar, water, and salt.
2. Bring to a boil and cook until the sugar syrup reaches 240° on a candy thermometer.
3. While the sugar syrup is cooking, beat egg whites with cream of tartar until stiff, gradually beat in confectioners sugar.
4. Pour hot syrup slowly over beaten egg whites, beating as you pour.
5. Add vanilla and continue beating until stiff peaks form.
6. Spread between, on top, and sides of cooled cake layers.

LADY BALTIMORE FROSTING
Fills and frosts 9 inch layer cake

1 recipe of fluffy white frosting
⅓ cup pecans, chopped
⅓ cup dates, chopped

⅓ cup maraschino cherries, drained and chopped
⅓ cup seedless raisins

1. To ⅓ of the fluffy white frosting add nuts, dates, cherries, and raisins.
2. Mix well and spread between layers.
3. Spread remaining frosting on top and sides of the cake.

BAKED HAM
Serves 8

6 to 8 pound cured ham or   **¼ cup brown sugar**
   part of ham   **Whole cloves**

1. Remove skin from ham.
2. Score fat. (Cut into fat diagonally from two directions.)
3. Pat brown sugar onto ham surface, stud with cloves.
4. Place ham in brown grocery bag and close securely.
5. Place in pan and bake at 350°, allow 20 minutes for each pound.
6. Remove from oven and let cool slightly before slicing.

Leftover ham is good for sandwiches, ham curry and ham fried rice.

HAM FRIED RICE
Serves 6

2 tablespoons bacon drippings   **3 cups cooked rice**
1 cup chopped onion   **2 cups diced cooked ham**
1 cup chopped bell pepper   **1 egg, beaten**
1 cup chopped celery

1. In heavy saucepan, sauté onion, pepper and celery in bacon drippings until tender but not brown.
2. Add ham and stir for several minutes.
3. Add rice and cook until rice is lightly browned.
4. Add beaten egg and stir in thoroughly.
5. Serve immediately.

Serve with soy sauce and a nice fruit salad.

HOBO STEW
Serves 4

1 pound hamburger
1½ teaspoons salt
Dash of pepper
1 10-ounce can tomato soup

3 carrots
3 medium potatoes
2 onions
2 cups water

1. Mix hamburger and ½ teaspoon salt.
2. Form into 1 inch meat balls.
3. Brown in 2 tablespoons oil in frying pan.
4. Peel, wash and quarter the carrots, potatoes, and onions.
5. In heavy saucepan mix tomato soup, water, 1 teaspoon salt, and pepper.
6. Heat to boiling; add vegetables and meat balls as they are browned.
7. Reduce heat, cover, and simmer for 45 minutes to 1 hour.

HUSH PUPPIES
Makes 2 dozen

¾ cup yellow corn meal
¼ cup flour
1 tablespoon cooking oil
2 teaspoons baking powder
½ teaspoon salt
2 tablespoons green pepper,
　finely chopped

2 tablespoons onion, finely
　chopped
½ cup milk
1 egg

1. Mix corn meal, flour, baking powder, salt, onion, and green pepper.
2. Stir in the egg, cooking oil, and milk; let stand until mixture begins to thicken.
3. Drop by the teaspoonful into hot oil in a deep fat cooker.
4. Cook until golden brown, turn and brown second side.
5. Serve hot with seafoods.

LASAGNA
Serves 6

1 quart spaghetti sauce
½ 8-ounce package egg
 noodles
1 8-ounce carton cottage
 cheese

1 6-ounce package Mozza-
 rella cheese
½ cup grated Parmesan
 cheese

1. Cover bottom of 2-quart oven proof casserole with ⅓ of the sauce.
2. Add ½ of the noodles (cooked according to direction on the package).
3. Add ½ of the cottage cheese, ½ of the mozzarella cheese, and sprinkle with ⅓ of the Parmesan cheese.
4. Cover with ⅓ of the sauce.
5. Make another layer of noodles and cheese; cover with remaining sauce.
6. Sprinkle with remaining ⅓ of Parmesan cheese.
7. Bake at 350° for 30 minutes or until lightly browned and bubbling.

MEAT LOAF
Serves 6

1½ pounds ground beef
1 cup Rice Krispies
1 small onion, chopped
½ 8-ounce can tomato sauce

1 egg, beaten
Dash pepper
1 teaspoon salt

Sauce:
½ 8-ounce can tomato sauce
2 tablespoons brown sugar
2 tablespoons prepared
 mustard

2 tablespons vinegar
1 cup water

1. Mix meat, Rice Krispies, onion, tomato sauce, egg, pepper, and salt.
2. Mix well and form into loaf.
3. Place in baking dish.
4. Mix all the sauce ingredients and pour over loaf in dish.
5. Bake at 325° for 1¼ hours, uncovered.

ONE, TWO, THREE, FOUR CAKE
Makes 2 or 3 9 inch layers

1 stick margarine
½ cup shortening
2 cups sugar
3 cups sifted flour
4 eggs

3 scant teaspoons baking
  powder
½ teaspoon salt
1 cup milk
1 teaspoon vanilla

1. Cream margarine, shortening, sugar, and vanilla until light and fluffy.
2. Add eggs one at a time, beating well after each.
3. Sift flour, salt, and baking powder together.
4. Add ½ of the flour at a time, alternating with the milk.
5. Divide equally between two or three 9 inch layer cake pans which have been greased generously and dusted with flour.
6. Bake at 325° for 20 minutes for 3 layers, 25 minutes for 2 layers.
7. Let stand for 10 minutes; turn out on racks to cool.
8. Frost with your favorite frosting.

This may be baked in a 9 inch tube pan. Bake at 325° for 1 hour, place on rack to cool before removing from pan.

When baking in a tube pan, 1 teaspoon lemon flavoring may be added along with the vanilla for a little different taste.

FRESH PEACH COBBLER
Serves 6

6 large, ripe peaches
½ cup sugar*
3 tablespoons tapioca

Dash of nutmeg
Dash of salt
2 tablespoons margarine

Crust:
1 cup self-rising flour
2 tablespoons sugar

¼ cup shortening
¼ cup milk

1. Peel and slice peaches.
2. Add sugar, tapioca, and nutmeg.
3. Stir lightly and set aside.
4. Cut shortening into flour and sugar.
5. Add milk and mix until flour is just dampened.
6. Pat out ot ¼ inch on a floured surface.

7. Cut into strips about 2 inches wide and line sides of 1-quart baking dish.
8. Carefully pour peach mixture into center of baking dish.
9. Dot with margarine.
10. Cut remaining dough with biscuit cutter and place rounds close together on top of peaches.
11. Sprinkle with a little sugar and nutmeg.
12. Bake at 400° for 10 minutes.
13. Reduce heat to 350° and bake 25 minutes longer.

*If peaches are not very sweet, add a little additional sugar.

PECAN PIE
Serves 8

½ cup sugar
1 cup white corn syrup
3 eggs, beaten
1 cup chopped pecans

2 tablespoons margarine
1 teaspoon vanilla
¼ teaspoon salt

1. Melt margarine, add sugar, syrup, eggs, nuts, vanilla, and salt.
2. Mix well.
3. Pour into *unbaked* 9 inch pie shell.
4. Bake at 300° for 1 hour.

PIE CRUST
Makes 1 pie shell

¼ cup shortening
2 tablespoons ice water

¼ teaspoon salt
¾ cup flour

1. Follow directions for double crust pie.
2. For pie shell prick unbaked crust.
3. Bake at 425° for 8 to 10 minutes until nicely browned; cool and fill according to directions for pie filling.
4. For unbaked pie shell do not prick, pour in filling and bake according to directions for filling.

PIE CRUST
Makes 1 pie crust and top

½ cup shortening
¼ cup ice water

½ teaspoon salt
1½ cups flour

1. Add salt to flour.
2. Cut shortening into flour until well blended.
3. Add water and stir until well mixed.
4. Roll out on well-floured counter until large enough to cover 9 inch pie pan. (Be careful not to work too much of the flour from the counter into the crust.)
5. Gently fit crust into pan, trim around edge of pan.
6. Pour in filling.
7. Roll remaining dough in same manner and place over filling.
8. Flute edge of crust and prick top; bake according to directions for filling.

PIZZA
Serves 6

2 cups self-rising flour
½ cup cooking oil
⅔ cup milk
8 ounces grated Mozzarella cheese

2 8-ounce cans tomato sauce
¼ teaspoon salt
Dash of pepper
1 teaspoon oregano

1. Mix flour, oil, and milk.
2. Stir until well blended; then knead on waxed paper.
3. Divide in half and place each half on a 10 inch pizza pan, dip your hand in flour and gently press dough out to fit the pan.
4. Sprinkle each pizza with ½ of the grated cheese.
5. Mix sauce, salt, pepper, and oregano. Spoon carefully over cheese.
6. Sprinkle remaining ½ of cheese over the sauce.
7. Top with any one or any combination of the following and bake at 375° for 20 to 25 minutes until golden brown and bubbly.

Sliced pepperoni
Sliced mushrooms
Chopped onion and green pepper
Crumbled bacon
Fried hamburger, crumbled

PIZZA PUPS
Makes 8

4 English muffins, split
1 pepperoni sausage sliced
  into thin slices

Pizza sauce
Grated Parmesan cheese

1. Spread muffins on cookie sheet.
2. Put one generous tablespoon of pizza sauce in center of each.
3. Lay slices of pepperoni on each.
4. Sprinkle generously with Parmesan cheese.
5. Bake at 375° for 10 to 12 minutes or until golden brown.

PIZZA SAUCE

1 8-ounce can tomato sauce
½ teaspoon oregano

Salt and pepper to taste

SHRIMP CREOLE
Serves 6

1 pound medium or small
  shrimp
1 medium onion, chopped
3 stems celery, chopped
1 medium green pepper,
  chopped

1 clove garlic, cut fine
1 6-ounce can tomato paste
2 No. 2 cans tomatoes
1 tablespoon oil
1 teaspoon salt
Dash of pepper

1. Wash and boil shrimp in a small amount of salted water about 15 minutes, cool, shell, and devein.
2. In heavy saucepan sauté onion, celery and green pepper in oil until tender but not brown.
3. Add all remaining ingredients except shrimp and simmer about 1 hour.
4. Add cooked shrimp and heat thoroughly.
5. Serve over cooked rice.

SHRIMP CURRY
Serves 6

¼ cup margarine
⅓ cup flour
1 teaspoon curry powder
1 cup milk

1 cup water
1 chicken bouillon cube
3 cups cooked shrimp
Salt and pepper to taste

1. Melt margarine in heavy saucepan.
2. Add flour and curry powder; stir in well.
3. Add milk, water, and bouillon cube and cook, stirring constantly until thickened.
4. Add cooked shrimp, salt, and pepper.
5. Serve hot over cooked rice.

Be sure to serve toasted coconut, or toasted slivered almonds with this dish.

SOUR CREAM POUND CAKE
Makes 1 9-inch Tube cake

1 stick butter
1 stick margarine
3 cups sugar
1 teaspoon vanilla flavoring
1 teaspoon lemon flavoring

6 eggs
3 cups plain flour
1 cup sour cream
¼ teaspoon soda

1. Cream butter, margarine, sugar, vanilla and lemon until light and fluffy.
2. Add eggs, 1 at a time, beating well after each.
3. Sift flour and measure, add soda and sift again.
4. Turn mixer to lowest speed and add flour alternately with sour cream, using ½ flour and ½ cream at each addition, mix well after each addition, but do not overbeat.
5. Pour into 9 inch tube pan that has been greased and floured, bake at 325° for 1 hour and 20 minutes.

SPAGHETTI SAUCE
Serves 6

1 pound hamburger
1 medium onion, chopped
3 stems celery, chopped
1 medium green pepper,
  chopped
1 clove garlic, cut fine

1 6-ounce can tomato paste
2 No. 2 cans tomatoes
1 tablespoon olive oil
1 teaspoon salt
Dash of pepper
½ teaspoon oregano

1. Heat oil in heavy frying pan.
2. Add meat and cook until brown, stirring so that meat breaks apart as it cooks.
3. Remove meat with slotted spoon and place in heavy saucepan.
4. Add onion, celery, green pepper, garlic, tomato paste, salt, pepper, oregano, and tomatoes.
5. Bring to boiling, reduce heat, and simmer for 1 to 2 hours.
6. Serve over cooked spaghetti, cooked according to directions on the package.

SPANISH BEEF RICE
Serves 4

½ pound ground beef
½ cup raw rice
½ small onion, chopped
½ small bell pepper, chopped
1 cup hot water

1 8-ounce can tomato sauce
½ teaspoon prepared
  mustard
½ teaspoon salt
Dash pepper

1. Brown meat, rice, onion, and pepper in heavy saucepan.
2. Add boiling water, tomato sauce, mustard, salt, and pepper.
3. Bring to a boil, cover, reduce heat and simmer, stirring occasionally, until rice is tender. About 25 minutes.

STRAWBERRY SHORTCAKE
Serves 6

1 cup self-rising flour
2 tablespoons shortening
2 tablespoons sugar
¼ cup milk
1 egg, beaten

8 oz. non-dairy whipped
  topping
1 pint of strawberries
½ cup sugar

1. Wash and remove stems from berries.
2. Place in a bowl and sprinkle with the ½ cup sugar.
3. Mix flour and sugar and cut in the shortening.
4. Stir in the milk and egg.
5. Press out on well-floured surface to about ½ inch thick.
6. Cut with biscuit cutter; place on ungreased baking sheet.
7. Bake at 425° for 10 to 12 minutes.
8. Split the cooled shortcakes and place the bottom half of each on a dessert plate.
9. Spread a little of the whipped topping on each; spoon sweetened berries over the topping.
10. Place the top half of the shortcake on top of the berries.
11. Spoon the remaining topping over the shortcake and top with remaining berries.

STRAWBERRY TARTS
Makes 8

1 pint fresh strawberries
½ cup sugar
1 tablespoon tapioca
1 tablespoon cornstarch

¼ teaspoon red food
  coloring
1 recipe pie crust for pie
  shell

1. Wash berries and remove stems, sprinkle with sugar, and let stand for 1 hour.
2. Drain juice into cup and add enough water to make ¾ cup.
3. Pour juice in saucepan and add tapioca, cornstarch, and red food coloring.
4. Cook, stirring constantly until thick and clear.
5. Cool and add berries.
6. Make tart shells with pie crust by rolling as usual and fitting into cups of muffin pan.
7. Bake at 425° for 5 to 8 minutes.
8. Spoon strawberry filling into cooled tart shells.
9. Top with sweetened whipped cream.

SWEDISH MEAT BALLS
Serves 4

1 pound hamburger
½ teaspoon salt
¼ teaspoon pepper
½ cup Rice Krispies
1 egg, beaten
½ cup milk
½ small onion, chopped

½ small bell pepper, chopped
1 8-ounce can tomato sauce
1 can chicken soup
1 cup water
¼ cup shortening

1. Mix meat, salt, pepper, Rice Krispies, egg and milk.
2. Shape meat mixture into small balls.
3. Saute onion and bell pepper in shortening until tender.
4. Heat soup, tomato sauce, water, onion, and bell pepper to boiling in a heavy saucepan.
5. Reduce heat and drop meat balls into cooking sauce, continue to simmer about 1 hour, covered.
6. Serve with buttered noodles.

SWISS STEAK
Serves 6

2 pounds round steak, cut
    into serving pieces
Salt and pepper
½ cup flour
½ cup cooking oil

1 cup tomato juice
3 medium potatoes
3 medium carrots
1 medium onion

1. Peel, wash, and cut vegetables into quarters.
2. Salt and pepper meat; dredge with flour.
3. Heat oil in heavy Dutch oven.
4. Quickly brown meat on both sides, remove meat from dutch oven, and pour off the drippings.
5. Return meat to pan, add potatoes, carrots, and onion.
6. Pour the tomato juice over the top and cover quickly.
7. Heat to boiling; reduce heat and simmer 1½ hours.

TOASTED COCONUT OR ALMONDS
Serves 6

1 cup Angel Flake coconut
    or slivered almonds

1. Spread evenly in shallow pan.
2. Bake at 300° until lightly browned.
3. Remove from oven and cool before serving.

Be careful not to burn; it browns *quickly.*

NOTES

All Stars

NOTES

BARBECUE SAUCE
Makes 1 pint

¾ cup cooking oil
¼ cup melted margarine
¼ cup lemon juice
1 tablespoon prepared mustard
2 tablespoons brown sugar
1 tablespoon salt
1 teaspoon paprika
¼ teaspoon pepper

1 tablespoon onion,
 chopped
2 cloves garlic, cut
½ teaspoon Worcestershire
 sauce
¼ teaspoon Tabasco sauce
¼ cup catsup

1. Put all ingredients into a pint container and shake well, or blend in blender.
2. Let stand for several hours for flavors to blend.

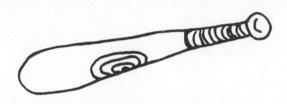

BREAD OR ROLLS
Makes 2 dozen rolls or 1 loaf of bread

1 package dry yeast
1 cup warm water
¼ cup sugar
1 teaspoon salt

3½ cups flour
1 egg, beaten
2 tablespoons margarine,
 melted

1. Dissolve yeast and sugar in warm water.
2. Add 2 cups flour and beat well.
3. Add beaten egg and melted margarine; mix well.
4. Add remaining flour and salt; stir until well mixed.
5. Knead several times on lightly floured surface.
6. Place in greased bowl; cover with towel.
7. Let rise in warm place until double in size.
8. Punch down, knead on floured surface and form into favorite rolls, cloverleaf, butterflake or caramel nut or into loaf.
9. Cover and let rise until double in size.
10. Bake at 400° for 12 to 15 minutes for rolls, 30 minutes for loaf of bread.

BRAISED SHORT RIBS
Serves 6 to 8

3 pounds short ribs
1 cup cooking oil
½ cup flour
1 teaspoon salt
Dash of pepper

1 medium onion, chopped
1 can golden mushroom
   soup
1 cup water
½ cup red wine

1. Salt and pepper ribs and dredge with flour.
2. Heat oil in heavy Dutch oven.
3. Brown ribs quickly in hot oil.
4. Remove ribs and pour off all but 2 tablespoons of oil.
5. Add remaining flour and brown stirring constantly.
6. Add water, soup, onions, and wine and stir well. (Be careful of the steam when adding water to hot pan.)
7. Return ribs to pan, stir well, cover tightly, heat to boiling, reduce heat, and simmer at least 1½ hours or longer.
8. Stir occasionally to keep from sticking.
9. Serve over hot buttered noodles.

A small can of sliced mushrooms, drained, may be added if desired.

STUFFED CABBAGE
Serves 6

1 pound hamburger
1 cup cooked rice
1 teaspoon salt
¼ teaspoon pepper
1 8-ounce can tomato sauce

1 small onion, chopped
1 cabbage with large leaves
1 cup canned tomatoes or
   tomato juice

1. Fry hamburger in heavy frying pan, stirring as it cooks to break apart.
2. When it is brown, use a slotted spoon to spoon it into a large bowl.
3. Add onion, salt, pepper, rice, and tomato sauce.
4. Mix well.
5. Wash cabbage and carefully separate leaves.
6. Line bottom of 2-quart casserole with heavy outside cabbage leaves.

7. Drop 6 cabbage leaves into boiling water until limp.
8. Remove from hot water and drain.
9. When the leaves are cool enough to handle, fill each leaf with the meat mixture.
10. Fold up the stem end, then each side, and last the end opposite the stem.
11. Place folded side down in baking dish.
12. Pour the tomatoes or tomato juice over the cabbage rolls. Cover tightly and bake at 350° for 1½ hours.

CARAMEL FUDGE
Makes 36 squares

3 cups sugar
⅔ cups milk
2 tablespoons butter

½ teaspoon vanilla
1 cup chopped nuts

1. Cook 2 cups sugar, milk and butter until it reaches a soft boil.
2. Keep warm over low heat.
3. In a dry heavy saucepan, brown 1 cup of sugar until light brown and melted.
4. Be careful not to burn.
5. When sugar has browned and turned to syrup pour slowly into cooked sugar and milk mixture, beating carefully as you pour.
6. Add vanilla and nuts and continue to beat until creamy, pour into well greased pan.
7. Cut into squares while still slightly warm.

CHEESE STRAWS OR WAFERS
Makes 4 to 5 dozen

1 stick margarine
6 ounces extra sharp Cheddar
  cheese, grated

1½ cups plain flour (sift before measuring)
Dash of Tabasco sauce

1. Cream margarine, grated cheese and Tabasco sauce until light and fluffy as whipped cream.
2. Slowly add flour and mix well.
3. Fill cookie press and form wafers or straws on ungreased cookie sheet.
4. Bake at 350° until lightly browned on bottom.

The secret of these is to beat margarine and cheese well and be careful not to overcook. Use a spatula to raise wafer and check bottom for browning.

These may be rolled into small balls by hand and pressed out flat if you do not have a cookie press.

BARBECUE CHICKEN
Serves 4

1 3-pound broiler-fryer,
  cut into quarters

1 teaspoon salt

1. Wash and drain chicken, sprinkle with salt, and let stand 1 hour.
2. Brush with barbecue sauce, let stand while charcoal is getting hot.
3. Place barbecue rack about 1 foot above coals, place chicken on rack and broil turning and brushing with additional sauce every 15 minutes until nicely browned and cooked thoroughly. At least 1 hour and 30 minutes.

CHICKEN AND DUMPLINGS
Serves 6

1 3-pound broiler-fryer, cut up   **1 chicken bouillon cube**
1 teaspoon salt   **1 quart water**

1. Wash chicken.
2. Place in large saucepan with water, salt, and bouillon cube.
3. Bring to boiling, reduce heat, and simmer until tender, at least 1 hour.
4. When chicken is tender, remove to another saucepan and add about ½ cup of stock; cover and place on warm to keep hot.

DUMPLINGS

2 cups self-rising flour   **¾ cup milk**
½ cup shortening

1. Cut shortening into flour.
2. Add milk and stir until flour is just dampened.
3. Drop by teaspoonfuls into simmering stock.
4. Cook without covering for 10 minutes.
5. Cover and cook 10 minutes longer.
6. Serve hot, using stock for gravy.

FRIED CHICKEN
Serves 6

1 2½-pound broiler-fryer,   **1 egg, beaten**
   cut up   **1 cup flour**
1 teaspoon salt   **2 cups cooking oil**
Dash pepper

1. Wash and drain chicken.
2. Salt and let stand about 1 hour.
3. Beat egg in large bowl, add chicken, and mix well.
4. Put flour and pepper in plastic bag.
5. Drop the chicken into the bag, 2 or 3 pieces at a time, and shake well; continue until all chicken is floured.
6. Heat oil in 10 inch heavy frying pan.
7. When oil is hot enough to sizzle when a little flour is dropped in, add the chicken carefully.

8. Reduce heat and cook until lightly brown, about 10 to 15 minutes.
9. Turn heat up, turn chicken over, reduce heat, fry until golden brown on second side, about 10 to 15 minutes.
10. When golden brown, remove from pan at once and drain on absorbent towels.
11. Serve hot.

HAWAIIAN CHICKEN
Serves 6

1 3-pound broiler-fryer, cut up	1 cup Kraft barbecue sauce
1 teaspoon salt	1 cup crushed pineapple
1 cup flour	1 tablespoon cornstarch
2 cups cooking oil	½ teaspoon ground ginger

1. Wash and drain chicken, salt and let stand about 1 hour.
2. Put flour in plastic bag, drop in chicken, 2 or 3 pieces at a time, shake well; continue until all chicken is floured.
3. Heat cooking oil in heavy 10 inch frying pan.
4. When oil is hot add the chicken and brown lightly on both sides, cook only long enough to brown.
5. Place browned chicken in a 12x8x2 inch casserole.
6. Mix pineapple, barbecue sauce, cornstarch and ginger.
7. Spoon over browned chicken, cover tightly with foil and bake at 350° for 1 hour. Remove foil and return to oven for 10 minutes.

CHICKEN PIE
Serves 6

¼ cup onion, chopped
¼ cup shortening
¼ cup flour
2 cups chicken stock
½ cup sliced cooked carrots

½ cup chopped cooked onion
½ cup cooked peas
¼ cup sliced cooked celery
2 cups cubed cooked
　chicken

1. Melt shortening and sauté onion until tender and lightly browned.
2. Remove ½ of the onion to small bowl.
3. Add flour to remaining onion and shortening; stir in well.
4. Add chicken stock and cook, stirring constantly until thickened.
5. Add carrots, peas, celery, onion and chicken; mix well.
6. Pour into 2-quart baking dish. Top with biscuit topping and bake at 375° about 20 minutes, until biscuits are lightly browned.

BISCUIT TOPPING

1½ cups self-rising flour
⅓ cup shortening

½ cup milk
Reserved onions

1. Cut shortening and onions into flour.
2. Add milk and stir until flour is just dampened.
3. Press out on well floured surface and cut with biscuit cutter.
4. Carefully lay biscuits on top of chicken mixture.

CHINESE PEPPER STEAKS
Serves 6

1 pound round steak, sliced
  into thin strips
1 small onion, sliced
1 cup celery, sliced
3 large green peppers, cut
  in slices
1 teaspoon salt

⅛ teaspoon pepper
1 clove garlic, cut very fine
2 cups water
2 beef bouillon cubes
¼ cup cornstarch
1 tablespoon soy sauce
¼ cup cooking oil

1. Brown meat in hot oil.
2. Add browned meat to 1½ cups water, bouillon cubes, salt and pepper in heavy saucepan. Cover, bring to boiling, reduce heat, and simmer for 15 minutes.
3. Add onion, celery, green peppers, and garlic. Cover and simmer 10 minutes.
4. Mix remaining ½ cup water with cornstarch and soy sauce, stir into meat and vegetables, cook, stirring constantly until thickened.
5. Serve over buttered cooked noodles.

DEVILED CRAB
Serves 6

½ stick margarine
½ small onion, chopped
½ bell pepper, chopped
1 stem celery, chopped
3 eggs, beaten
12 Ritz crackers, crumbled
  slightly
1 heaping tablespoon
  mayonnaise

1 teaspoon prepared
  mustard
1 tablespoon Worcestershire
  sauce
1 dash Tabasco sauce
½ teaspoon salt
Black pepper
¼ cup milk
1 pound claw crab meat

1. Melt margarine in heavy saucepan.
2. Sauté onion, celery, and pepper until tender, but not browned.
3. Beat eggs, add all other ingredients, and toss together lightly until well mixed.
4. Turn into 1-quart casserole, sprinkle with additional cracker crumbs, and paprika.
5. Bake at 325° about 25 to 30 minutes or until firm.

DIVINITY
Makes 36 pieces

½ cup water
½ cup white corn syrup
2½ cups sugar

2 egg whites
½ cup chopped nuts
1 teaspoon vanilla

1. Mix water, syrup, and sugar in saucepan.
2. Bring to a hard boil (260° on a candy thermometer).
3. While this is cooking, beat egg whites until very stiff.
4. Pour cooked syrup over stiffly beaten egg whites, continuing to beat while pouring the syrup.
5. Beat until candy begins to hold its shape.
6. Add vanilla and nuts, mix in well, and drop by the teaspoonful on greased cookie sheets. Let stand until firm.

This candy should stand up just as it falls from the teaspoon. If it does not, it is not cool enough to drop.

LEMON MERINGUE PIE
Serves 8

1 package Jello lemon pudding and pie filling (not instant)
⅔ cup sugar
2 cups water
2 tablespoons lemon juice

2 tablespoons margarine
3 eggs, separated
6 tablespoons sugar

1. Cook pudding according to directions on package, using ⅔ cup sugar, 2 cups water, and 3 beaten egg yolks.
2. Cool slightly; add margarine and lemon juice, mix well.
3. Pour into 9 inch *baked* pie shell.
4. Top with meringue and bake at 300° for 30 minutes.

MERINGUE

1. Beat 3 egg whites until peaks begin to form.
2. Gradually add 6 tablespoons sugar and continue beating until very stiff.

PARTY OYSTERS
Serves 6 to 8

½ pint raw oysters, medium
size

Sliced bacon cut into thirds
Salt and pepper

1. Be sure oysters are free of shell, and rinse lightly.
2. Wrap each oyster in a third of a slice of bacon, and pin with a toothpick.
3. Place on broiler pan, and sprinkle lightly with salt and pepper.
4. Broil until bacon is lightly browned, turning once.
5. Serve at once with cocktail sauce for dipping.

PEAS AND POTATOES
Serves 6

6 medium potatoes
1 10-ounce package green peas
1 can cream of mushroom
soup

1 teaspoon salt
Pepper to taste

1. Peel, wash and cut potatoes into quarters.
2. Boil potatoes and peas in salted water until tender.
3. Drain all but about 1 cup of water.
4. Add mushroom soup, pepper to taste and mix well.

STUFFED PEPPERS
Serves 6

1½ pounds hamburger
1 small onion, chopped
1 cup Rice Krispies
1 egg, beaten
1 cup milk

1 teaspoon salt
¼ teaspoon pepper
1 8-ounce can tomato sauce
6 bell peppers, medium size

1. Wash peppers, cut off tops, and remove seeds.
2. Mix hamburger, onion, Rice Krispies, egg, milk, salt, and pepper.
3. Stuff each pepper with the meat mixture.
4. Stand each pepper in a baking dish.
5. Pour tomato sauce over stuffed peppers.
6. Cover and bake at 350° for 1½ hours.

POT ROAST
Serves 6

3 to 4 pound chuck roast
1 cup cooking oil
½ cup flour
1 teaspoon salt
Pepper

4 medium potatoes
4 carrots
2 onions
1 cup tomato juice

1. Peel, wash, and cut potatoes, carrots, and onions in quarters.
2. Salt and pepper roast and rub flour into meat.
3. Heat oil in heavy Dutch oven.
4. Brown meat quickly on both sides.
5. Remove meat from pan and drain off most of the drippings.
6. Return meat to pan and add potatoes, carrots, and onions.
7. Add tomato juice.
8. Cover tightly and bring to a boil; reduce heat at once and simmer for at least 3 hours.

GRAVY

2 cups water
2 tablespoons cornstarch
(more if you like thicker gravy)

1. Remove meat to platter, and vegetables to serving bowl.
2. Add water to juices in Dutch oven and bring to a boil.
3. Reduce heat and gradually add the cornstarch which has been dissolved in ¼ cup water, stirring constantly until gravy is desired thickness.
4. Salt and pepper to taste.

FRENCH ONION POT ROAST
Serves 6

4 pound chuck roast
1 package dry onion soup
  mix
½ cup cooking oil

1 cup water
½ cup flour
1 teaspoon salt
Pepper

1. Sprinkle roast with salt and pepper.
2. Rub flour into all sides of the roast.
3. Heat oil in heavy Dutch oven.
4. Brown meat quickly on all sides in hot drippings.
5. Remove roast from pan and pour off all but a little of the drippings.
6. Return roast to pan; mix water and soup mix, pour over roast and cover quickly.
7. Bring to a boil, reduce heat at once, and simmer for 2½ to 3 hours.

To make gravy: Remove roast from pan, add 1 to 2 cups water to pan, heat to boiling. Thicken with 2 tablespoons cornstarch mixed in ¼ cup water added gradually, stirring constantly until gravy is desired consistency. You may need more cornstarch if you like thicker gravy.

QUICK BEEF PIE
Serves 6

1 recipe Monday's Hash
1 10-ounce package frozen
  mixed vegetables

2 tablespoons cornstarch

1. Cook mixed vegetables by directions on the package.
2. Drain vegetables and add to hash.
3. Mix cornstarch with a little water and slowly add to hash, stirring constantly until mixture is slightly thickened. (You may not need all the cornstarch.)
4. Pour into 2-quart casserole; top with biscuit topping and bake at 375° for 20 to 25 minutes until lightly browned.

BISCUIT TOPPING

1½ cups self-rising flour
½ cup shortening
½ cup milk

2 tablespoons onion, chopped

1. Sauté onion in a little of the shortening until they are tender and lightly browned.
2. Cut shortening and cooled onions into flour, stir in milk.
3. Press out on well floured surface and cut with biscuit cutter.
4. Carefully lay biscuits on top of beef mixture.

CHARCOAL BROILED CHUCK ROAST
Serves 6 to 8

3 pound chuck roast
½ cup onion flakes
2½ teaspoons salt

½ teaspoon black pepper
¾ cup red wine vinegar and oil dressing

1. Place roast and other ingredients in a heavy plastic bag.
2. Close tightly and refrigerate overnight, turning occasionally.
3. Remove from refrigerator about an hour before cooking.
4. Cook over hot charcoal on grill for approximately 40 minutes, turning several times.

ROLLS, Use 1 recipe of bread dough for each of these.

BUTTERFLAKE ROLLS
Makes 2 dozen

1. Grease two large, dozen size, muffin pans.
2. Divide dough in half and roll out on floured surface to about 8x12 inches.
3. Brush with melted butter.
4. Cut into four strips 2 inches wide.
5. Stack these one on top of the other.
6. Cut into 12 equal pieces.
7. Place each piece in a greased muffin cup.
8. Follow same directions with other half of dough.
9. Cover and let rise until double in size.
10. Bake at 400° for 12 to 15 minutes.

CARAMEL NUT ROLLS
Makes 2 dozen

1¼ cups brown sugar
½ cup melted margarine

¼ cup white corn syrup
1 cup nuts, chopped

1. Grease two large, dozen size, muffin pans.
2. Mix ¾ cup brown sugar, ¼ cup melted margarine, and ¼ cup corn syrup, and heat just enough to blend well.
3. Divide the brown sugar mixture equally between the 24 muffin cup.
4. Divide nuts equally between the 24 muffin cups.
5. Divide the dough in half; roll out on floured surface to about 8x12 inches.
6. Brush with 2 tablespoons of melted margarine and sprinkle with ¼ cup brown sugar; sprinkle with ground cinnamon.
7. Roll up like a jelly roll; cut into 12 equal pieces.
8. Place one cut piece in each muffin cup.
9. Follow same directions with second half of dough.
10. Cover and let rise until double in size.
11. Bake at 350° for 10 minutes, remove from oven, and turn out of pans at once.

CLOVERLEAF ROLLS
Makes 2 dozen

1. Grease 2 large, dozen size, muffin pans.
2. Divide dough in half and pinch off 36 equal pieces.
3. Roll into balls; place three balls in each muffin cup.
4. Follow same directions with second half of dough.
5. Cover and let rise until double in size.
6. Bake at 400° for 12 to 15 minutes.

SHISH KABOBS
Serves 6

2 pounds boneless chuck
  roast
½ cup cooking oil
1 package dry onion soup mix
⅓ cup cider vinegar or red
  wine
1 teaspoon salt

¼ teaspoon pepper
12 small potatoes
12 small salad tomatoes
12 canned onions
12 canned mushroom caps
1½ bell peppers, cut into
  12 pieces

1. Mix oil, soup mix, vinegar, salt, and pepper.
2. Cut meat into 1 inch cubes; put into glass bowl.
3. Pour oil mixture over meat, cover tightly and marinate in refrigerator at least 6 hours or overnight; stir several times.
4. Remove meat from refrigerator about 1 hour before cooking time.
5. Wash unpeeled potatoes well and boil for about 10 minutes.
6. Drain potatoes well.
7. Thread meat cubes on skewers alternately with potatoes, onions, tomatoes, mushrooms, and bell peppers.
8. Broil over hot charcoal on grill until done, brushing with remaining oil mixture as they cook.

¾ cup red wine vinegar and oil dressing may be used in place of the ½ cup cooking oil and ⅓ cup vinegar or red wine.

WORK YOUR WAY UP
INDEX

CLASSIFIED
INDEX

INDEX

NOTES

NOTES

Strictly For Boys
P.O. Box 474
Beaufort, South Carolina 29902

Please send _____ copies to:

Name _____

Address _____

City_____State_____Zip_____

Enclosed is $7.95 plus $1.25 postage and handling for each book ordered.
S.C. residents add 40¢ tax per book.

Strictly For Boys
P.O. Box 474
Beaufort, South Carolina 29902

Please send _____ copies to:

Name _____

Address _____

City_____State_____Zip_____

Enclosed is $7.95 plus $1.25 postage and handling for each book ordered.
S.C. residents add 40¢ tax per book.

Strictly For Boys
P.O. Box 474
Beaufort, South Carolina 29902

Please send _____ copies to:

Name _____

Address _____

City_____State_____Zip_____

Enclosed is $7.95 plus $1.25 postage and handling for each book ordered.
S.C. residents add 40¢ tax per book.

Re-Order Additional Copies